This Book Belongs To

_____

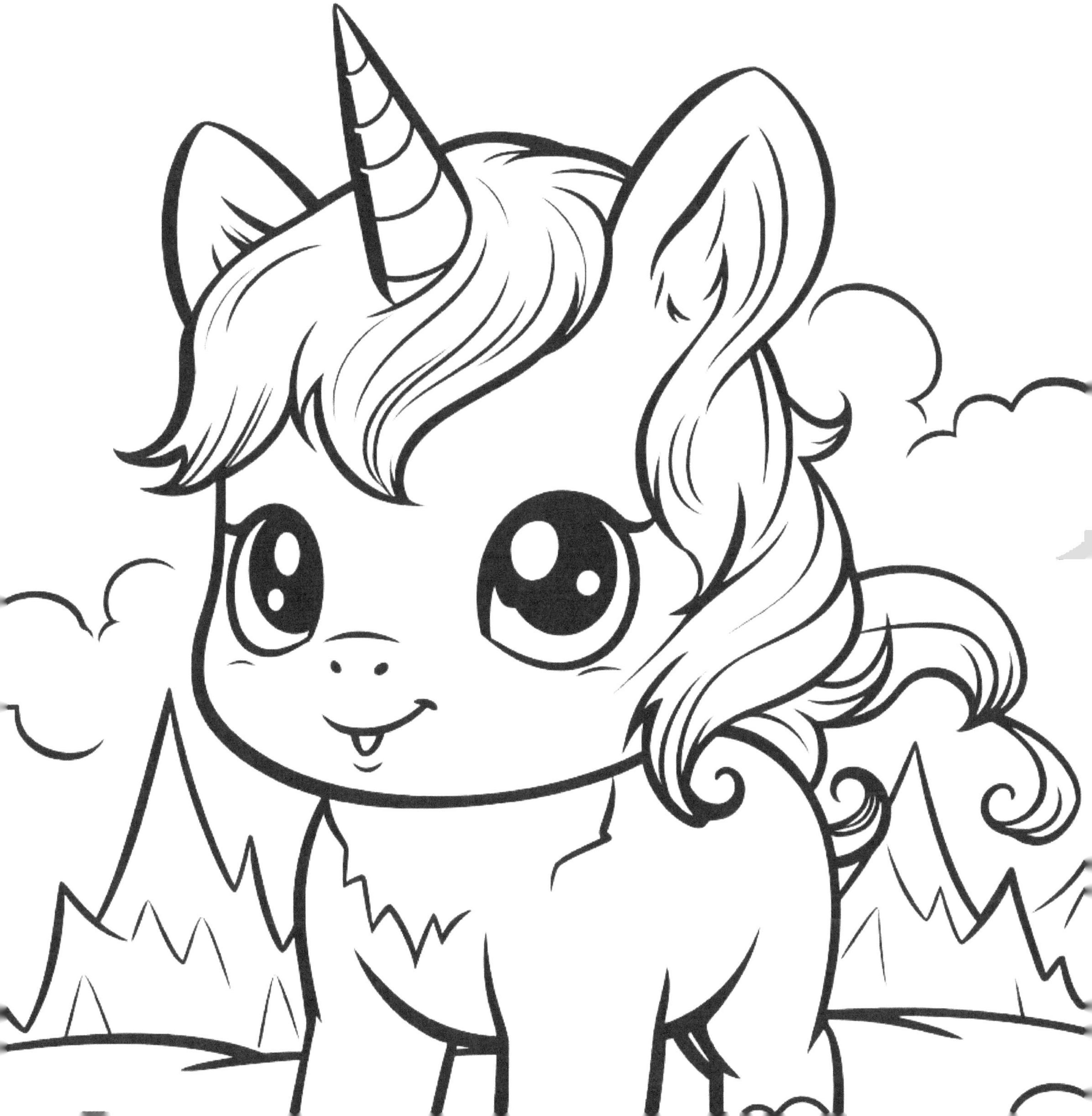

Aa Apple

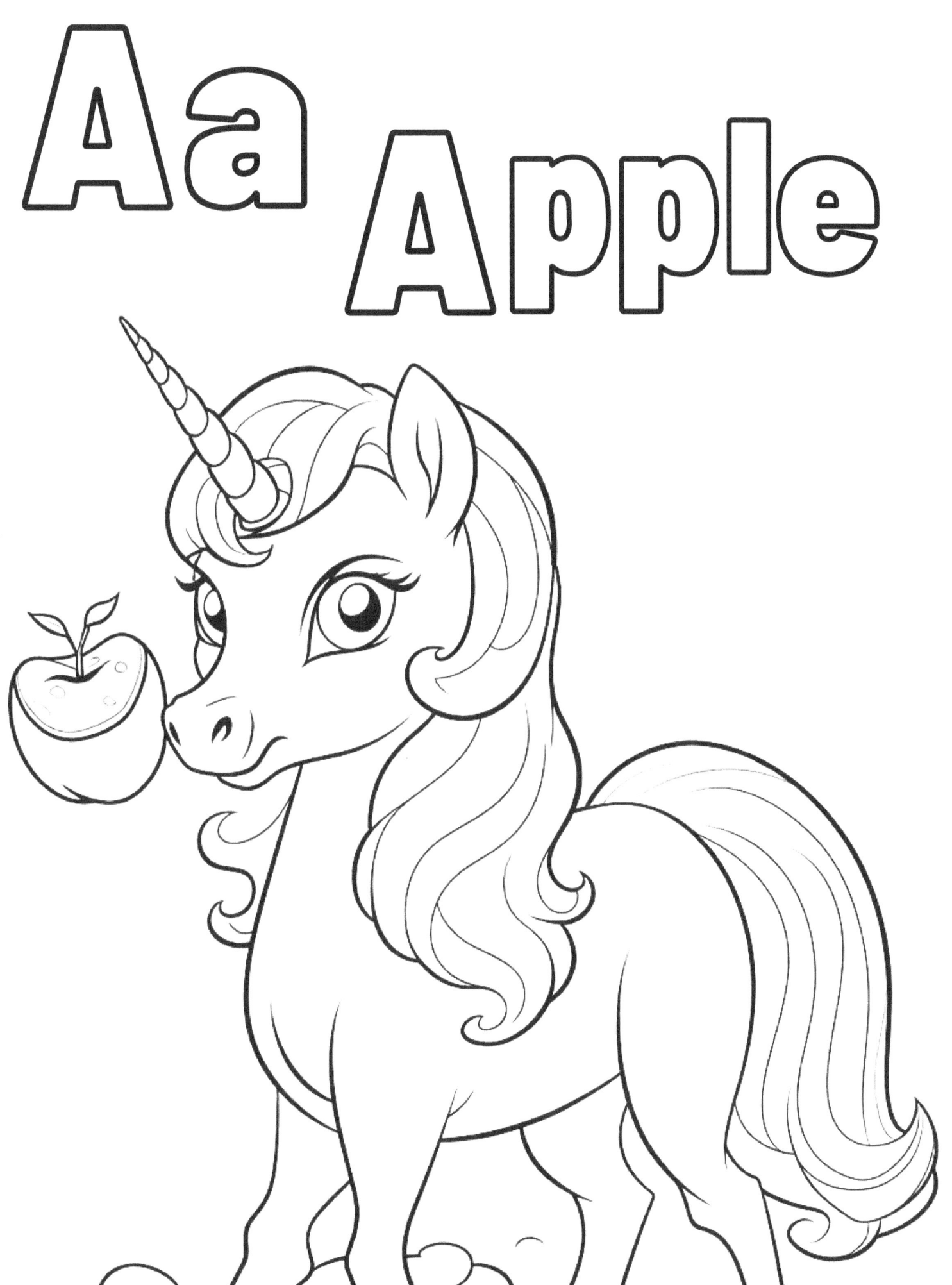

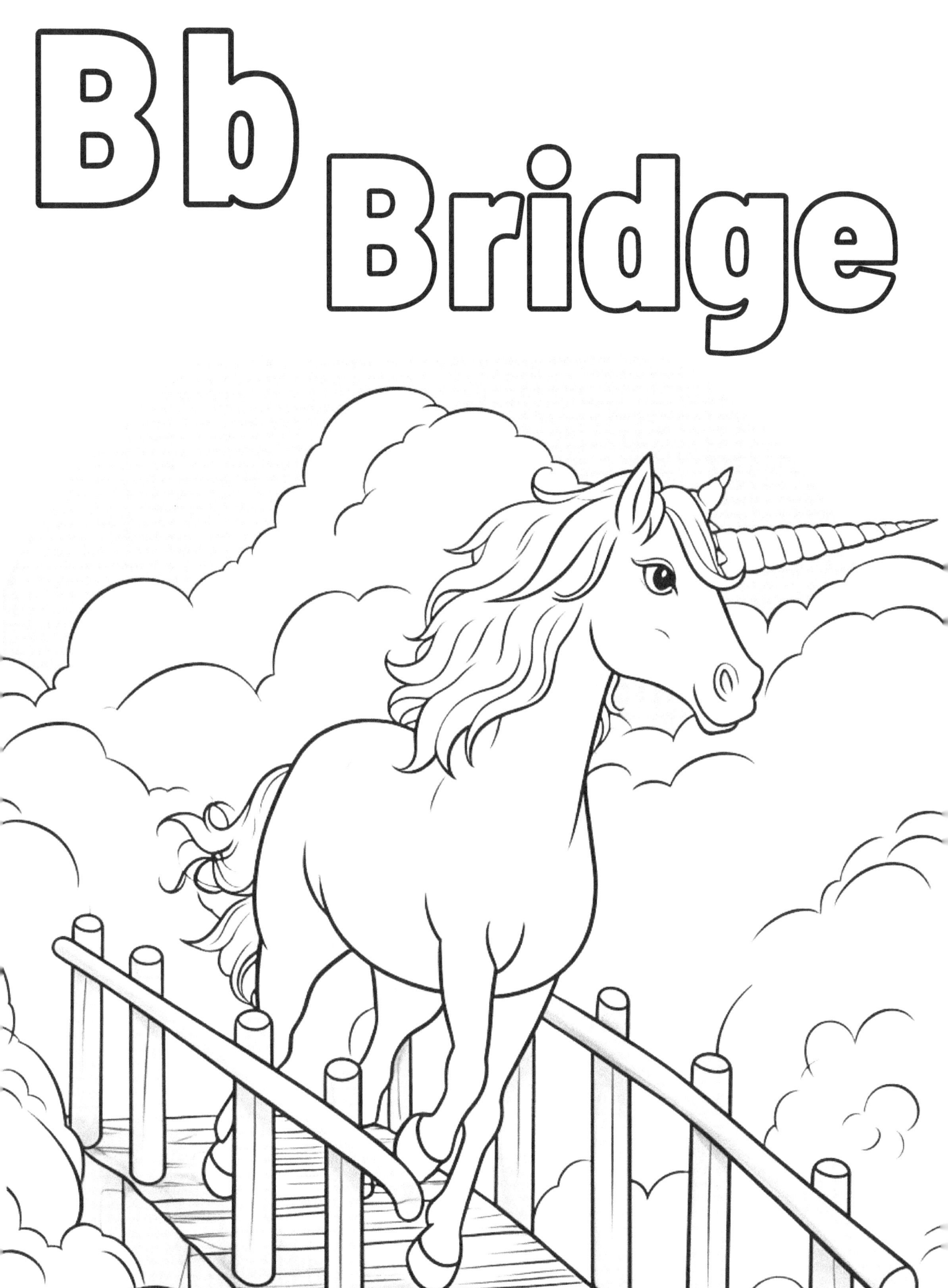

Cc   Car

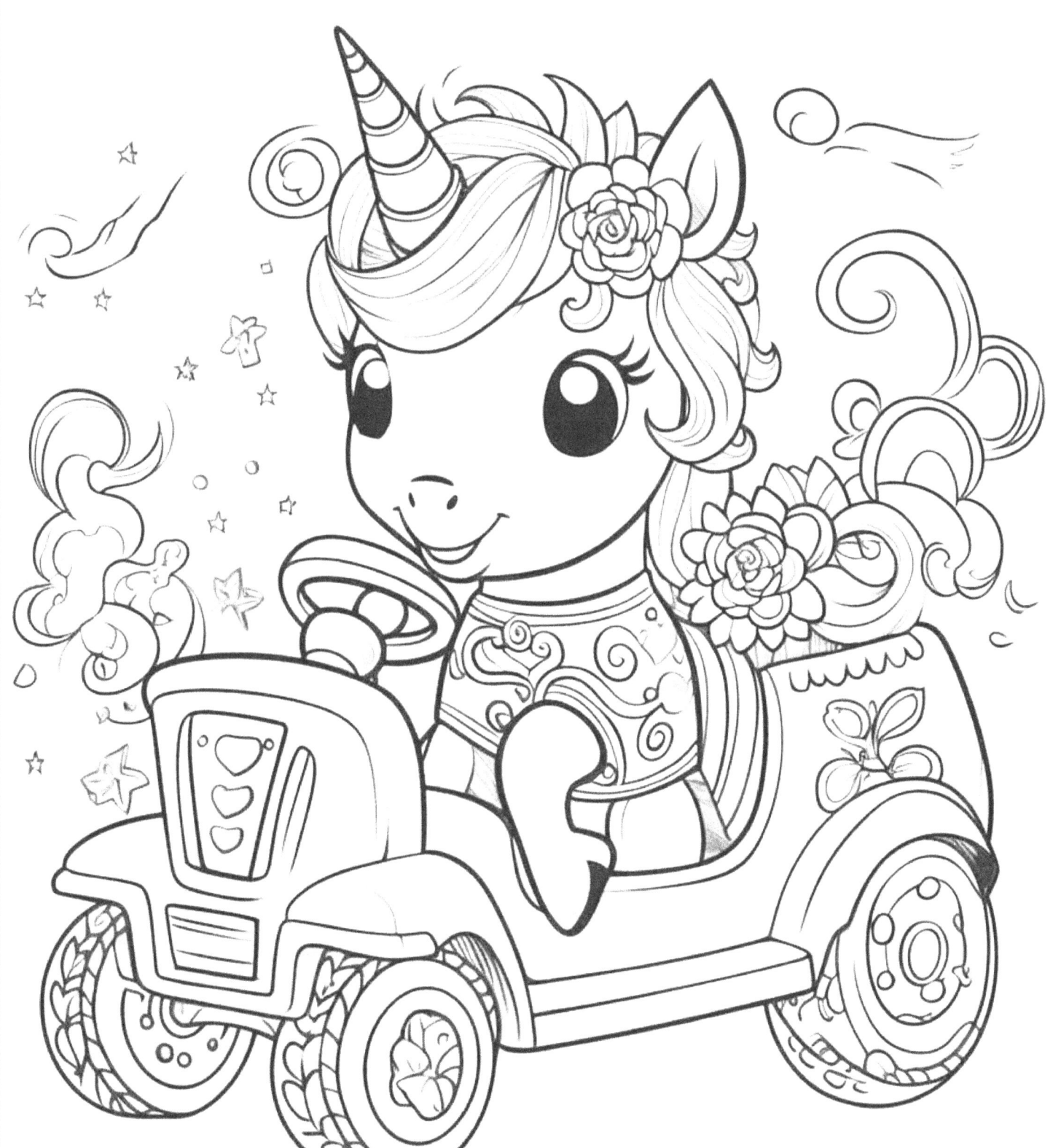

Dd Donut

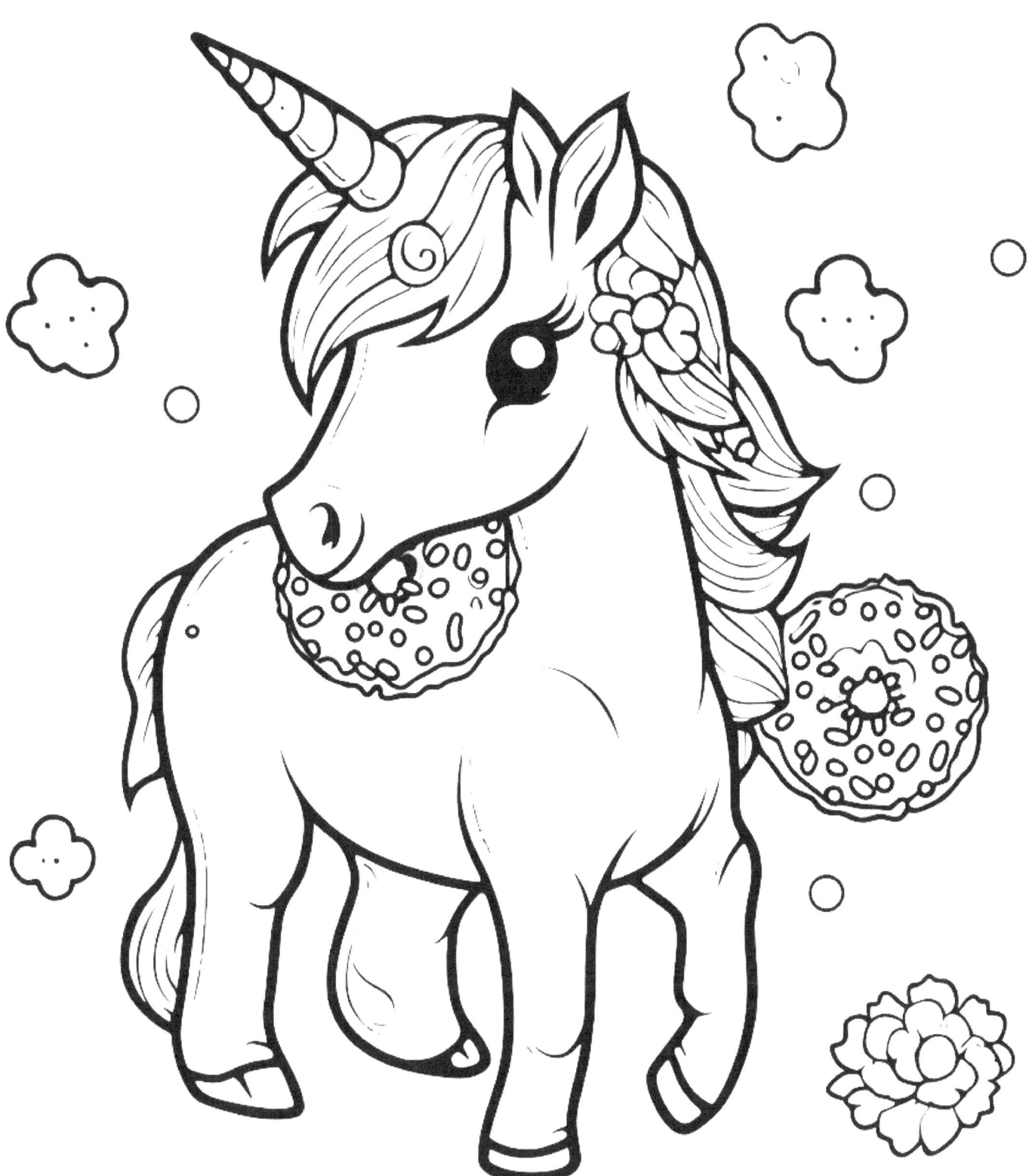

Ee   Egg

Ff Flower

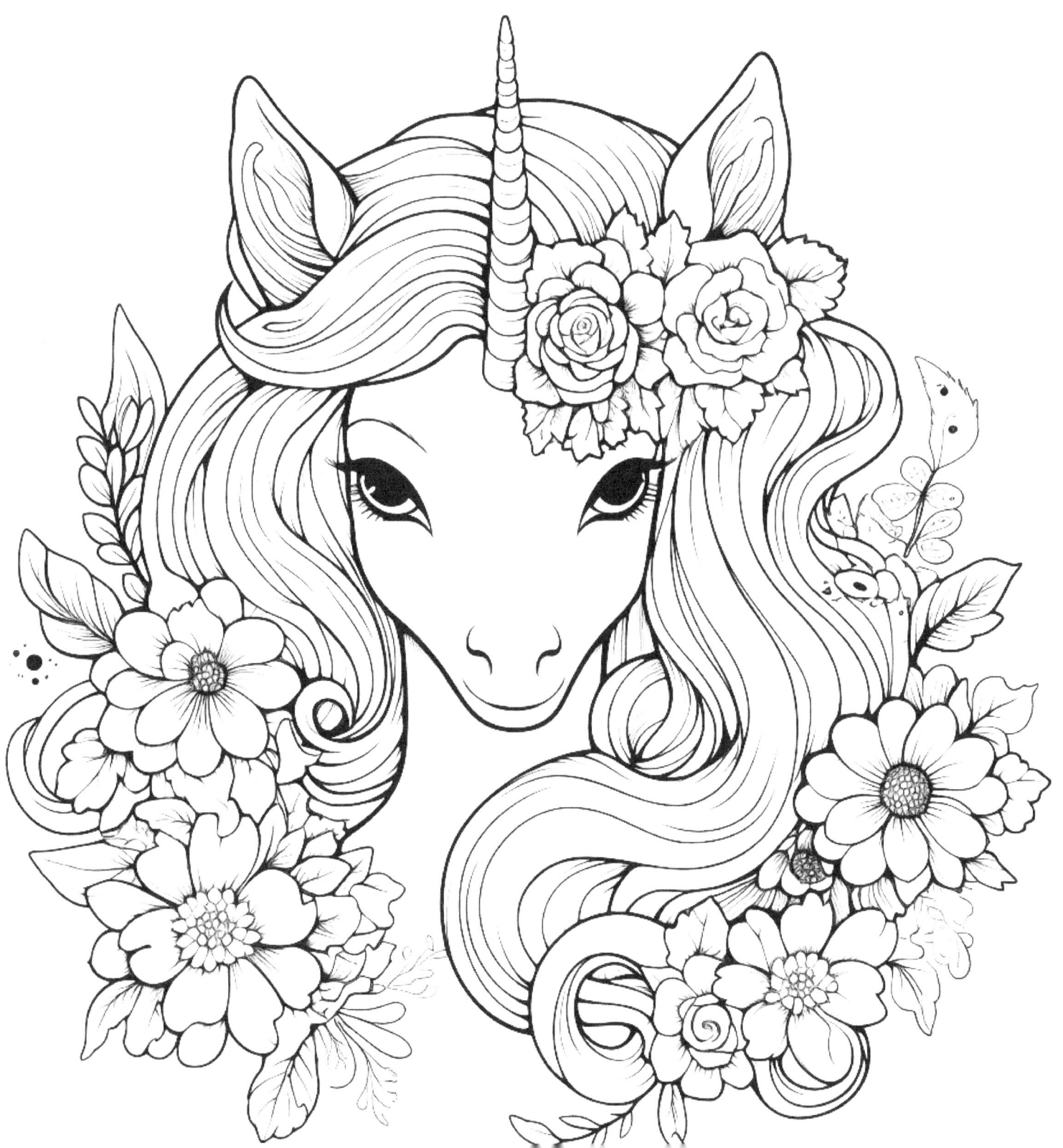

Gg Glasses

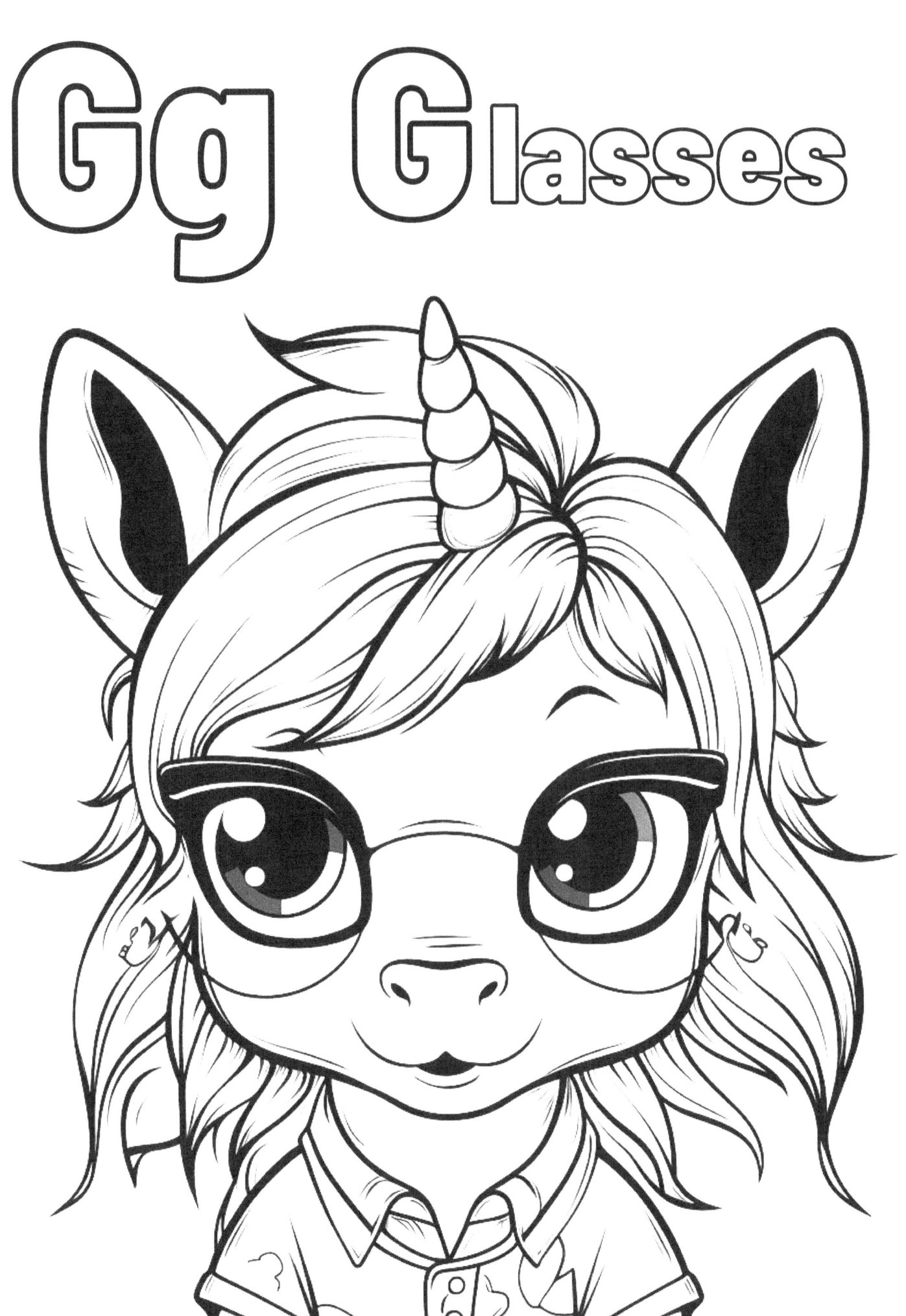

Hh House

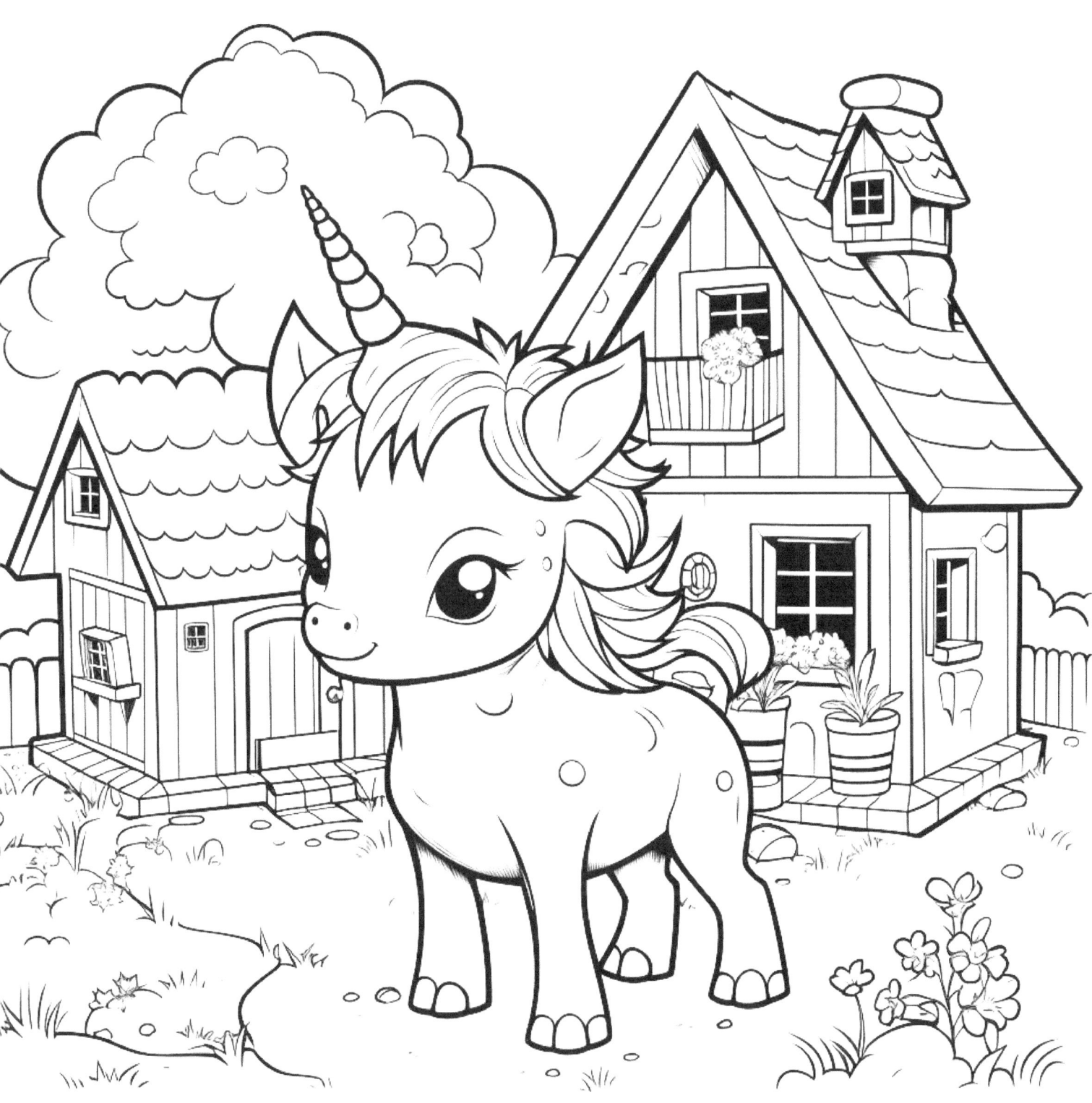

Ii   Ice

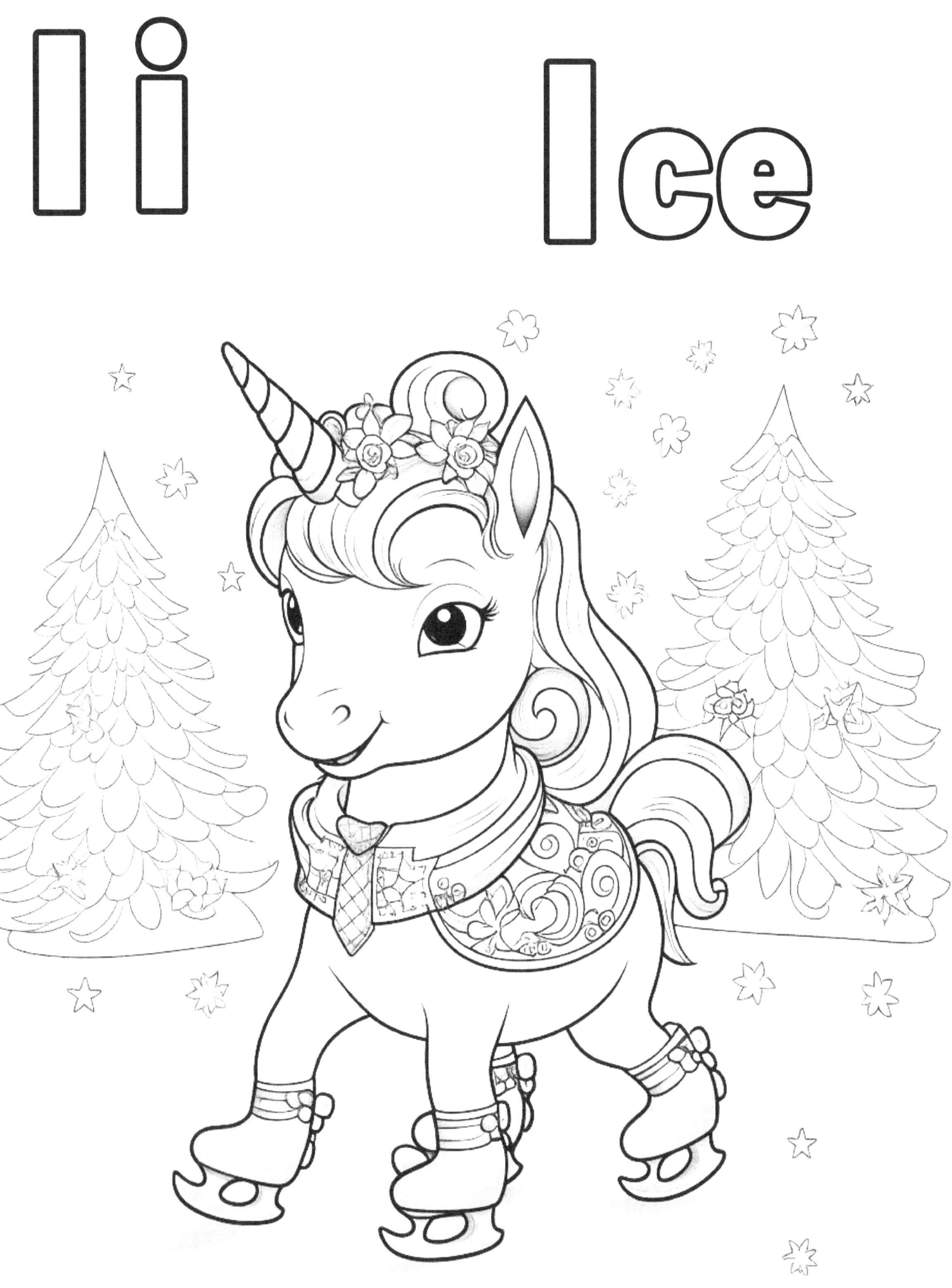

Jj   Jump

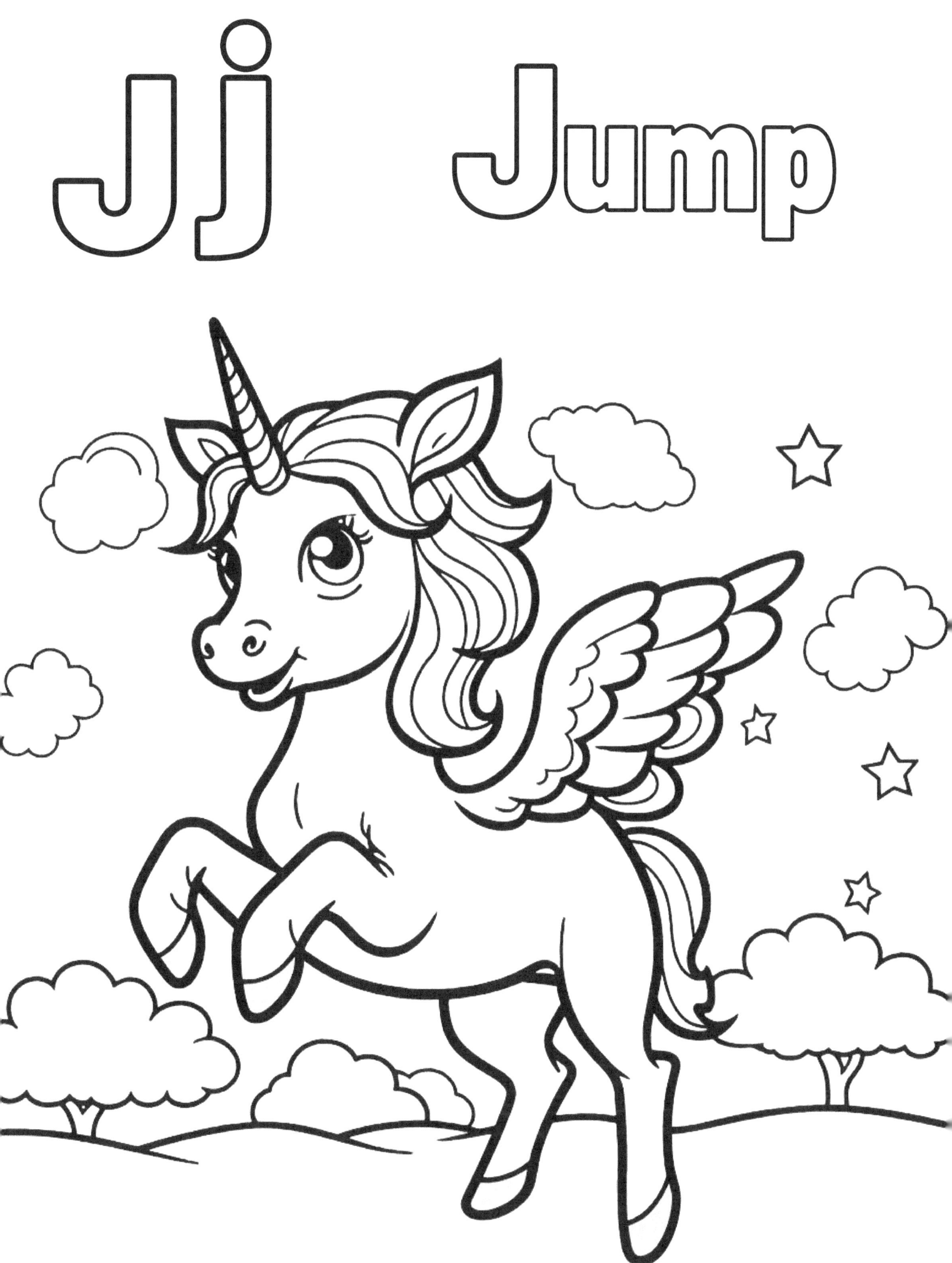

Kk King

Ll Love

Mm Morning

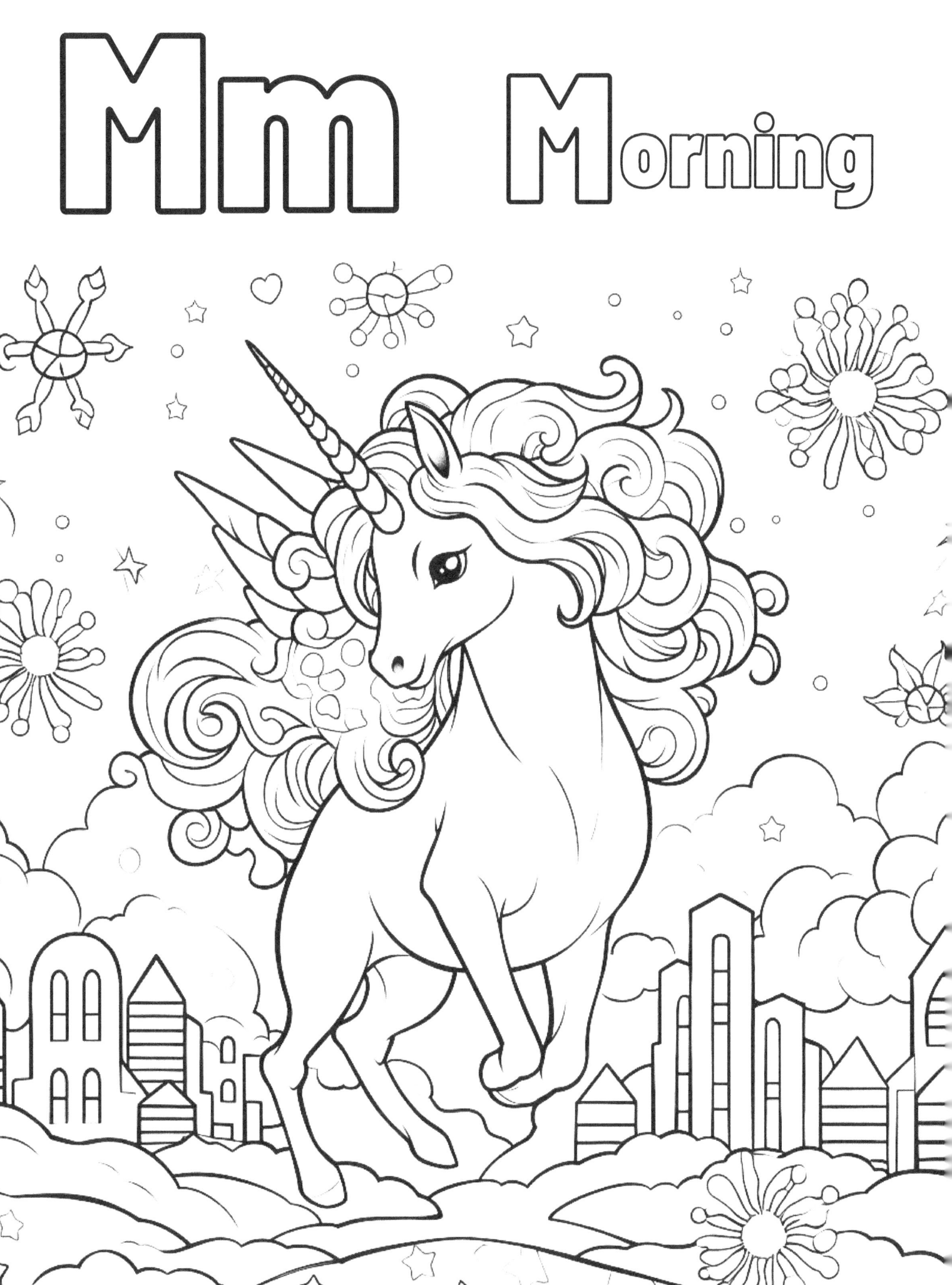

N n   Nap

Oo Orange

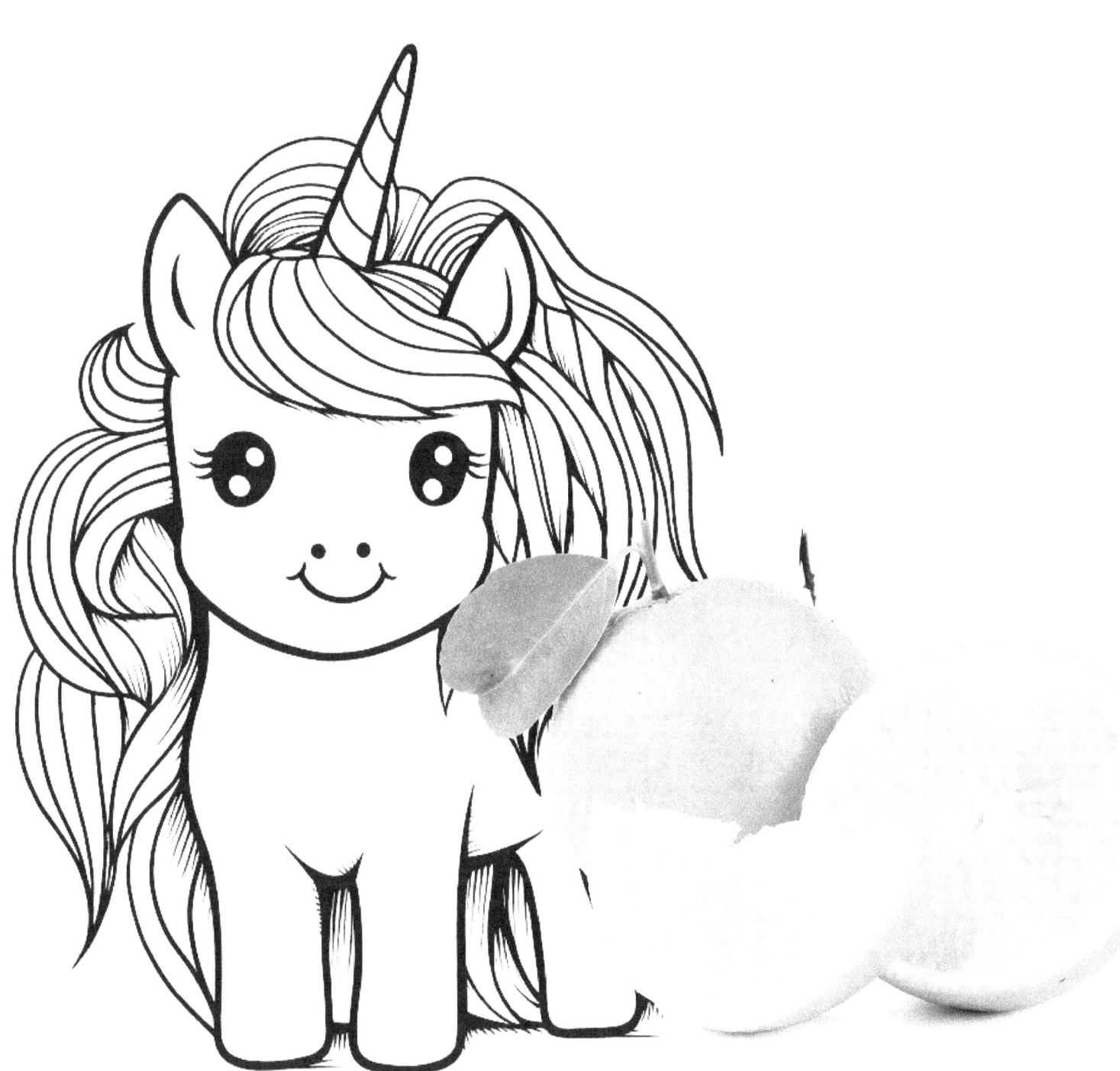

P p

Pig

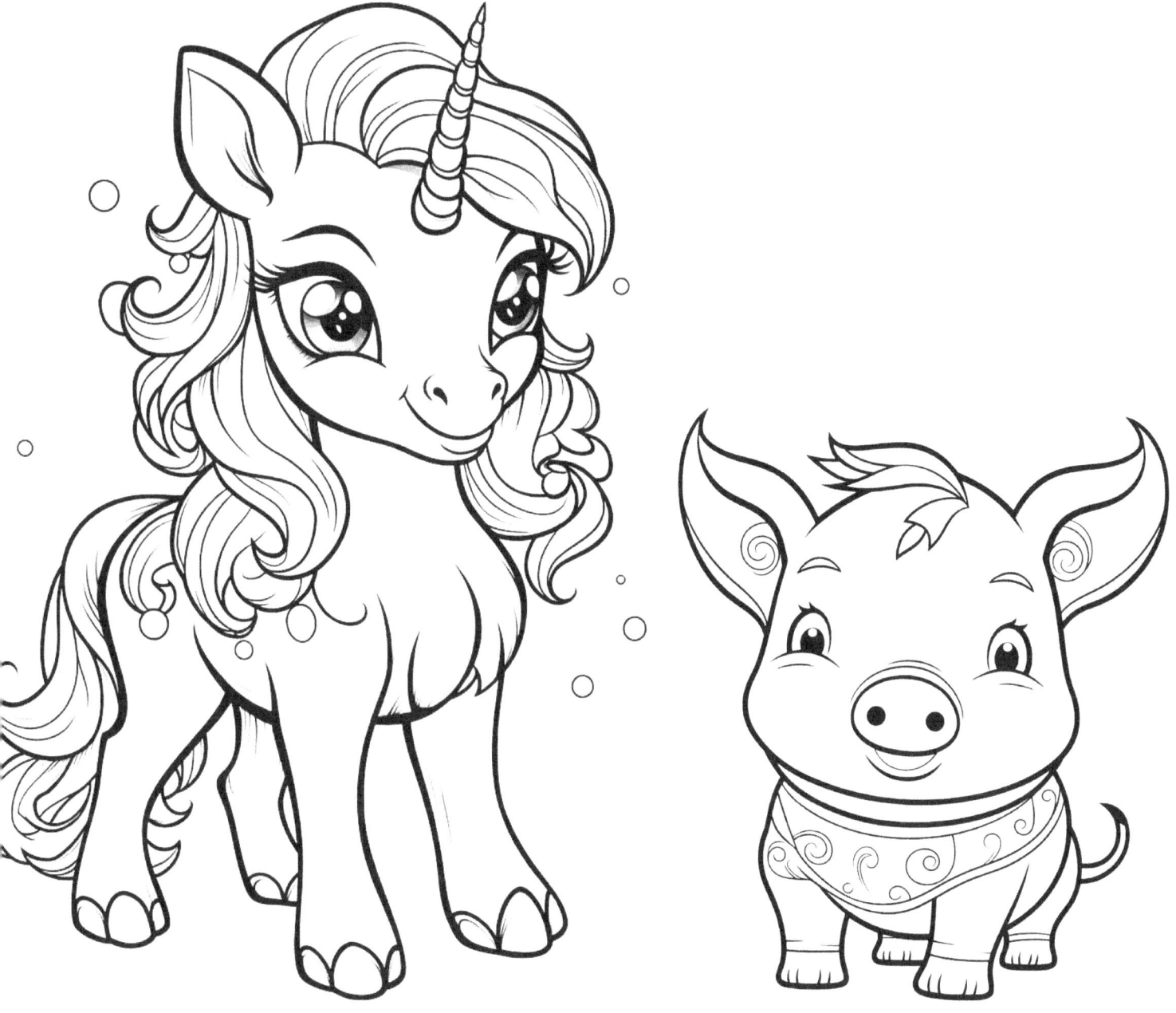

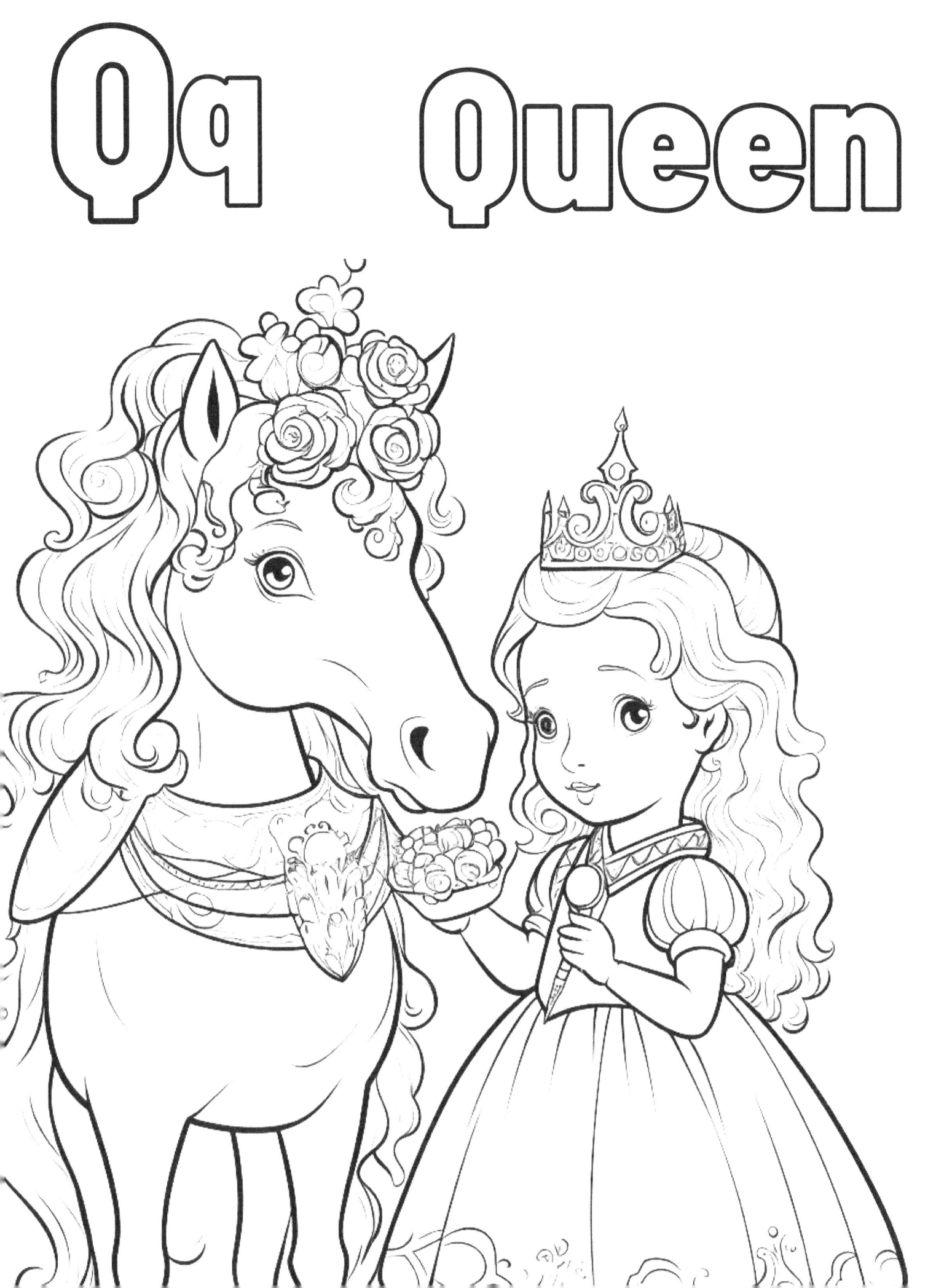

R r   Rain

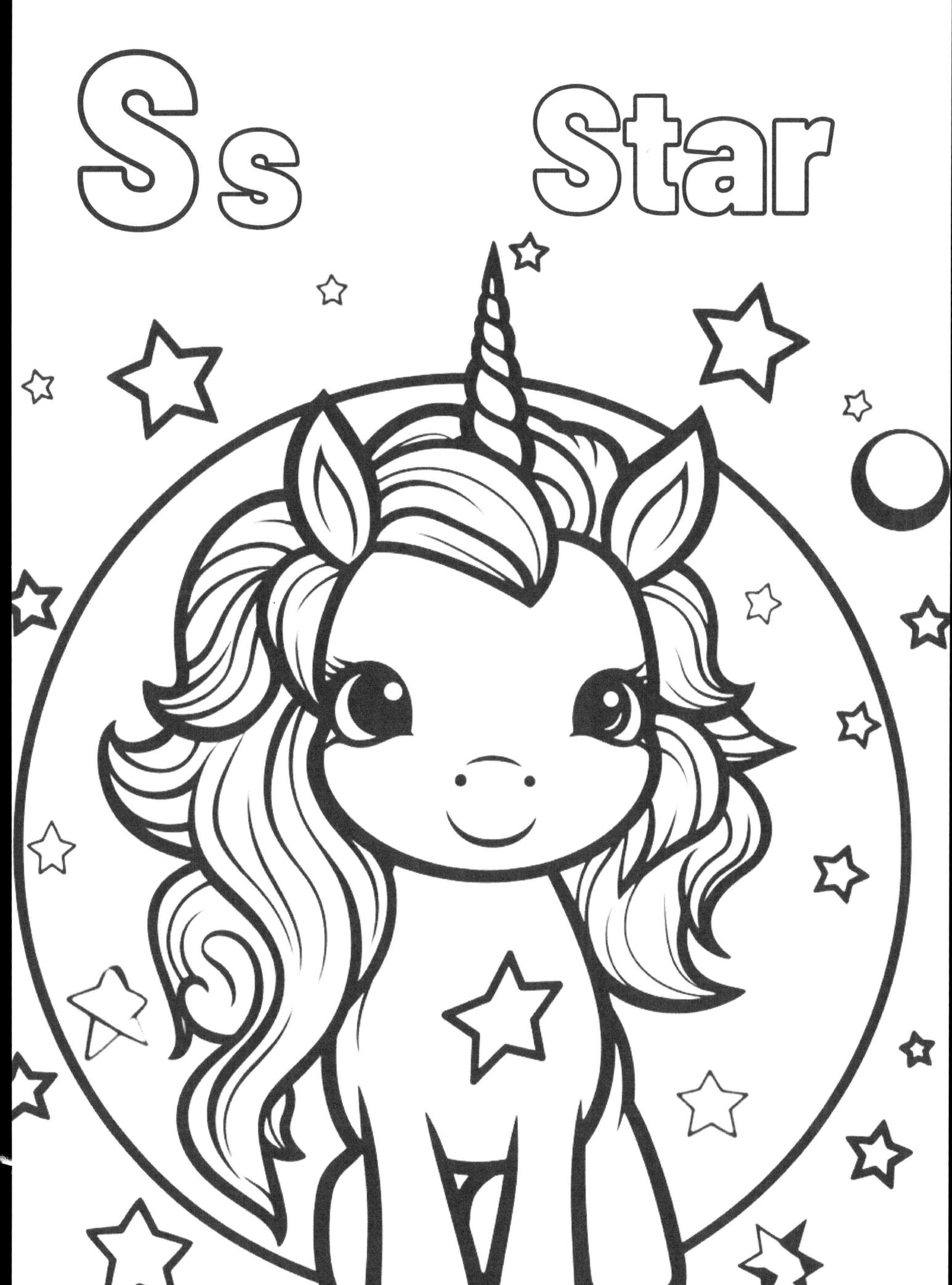

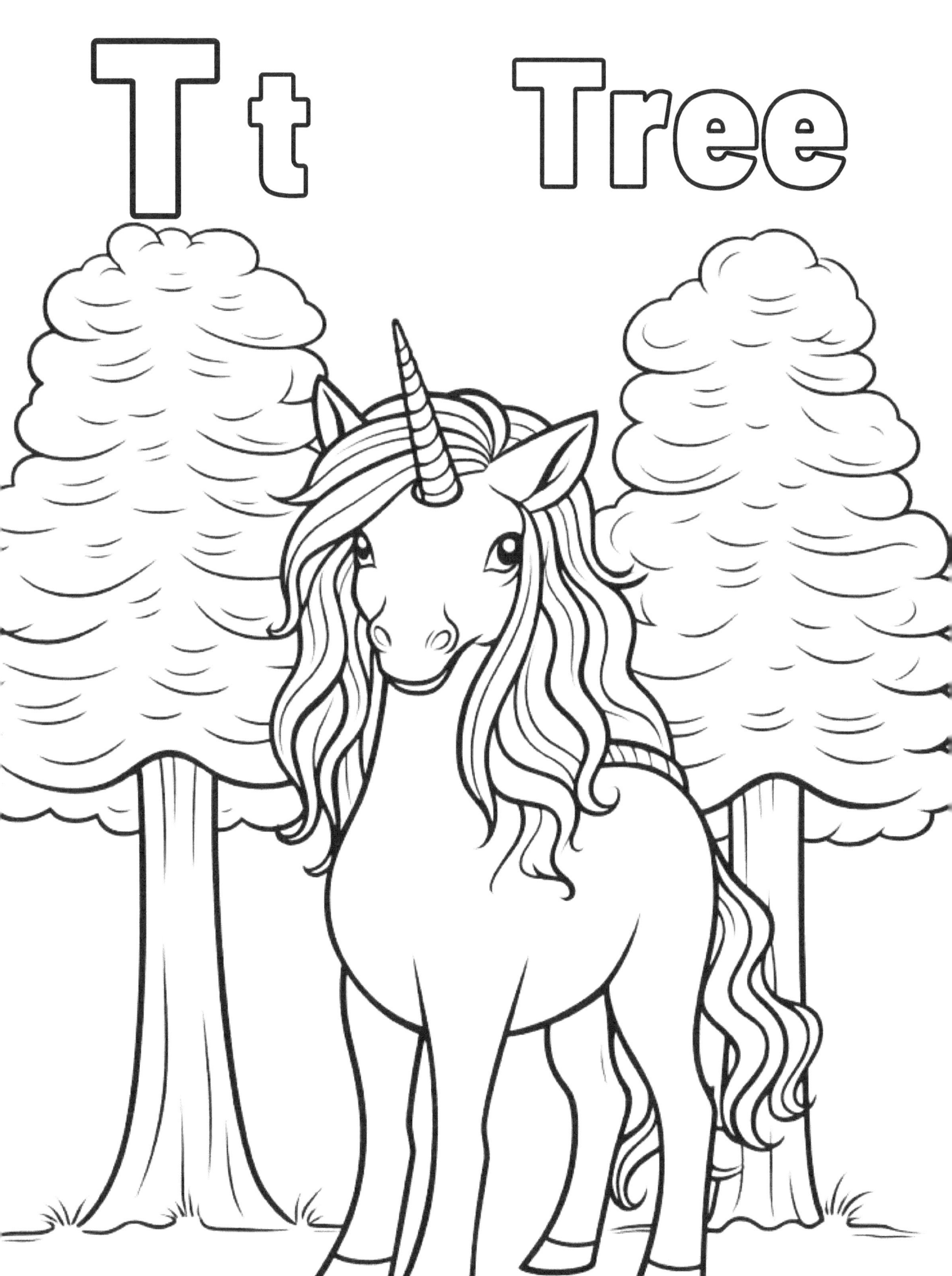

U u Unicorn

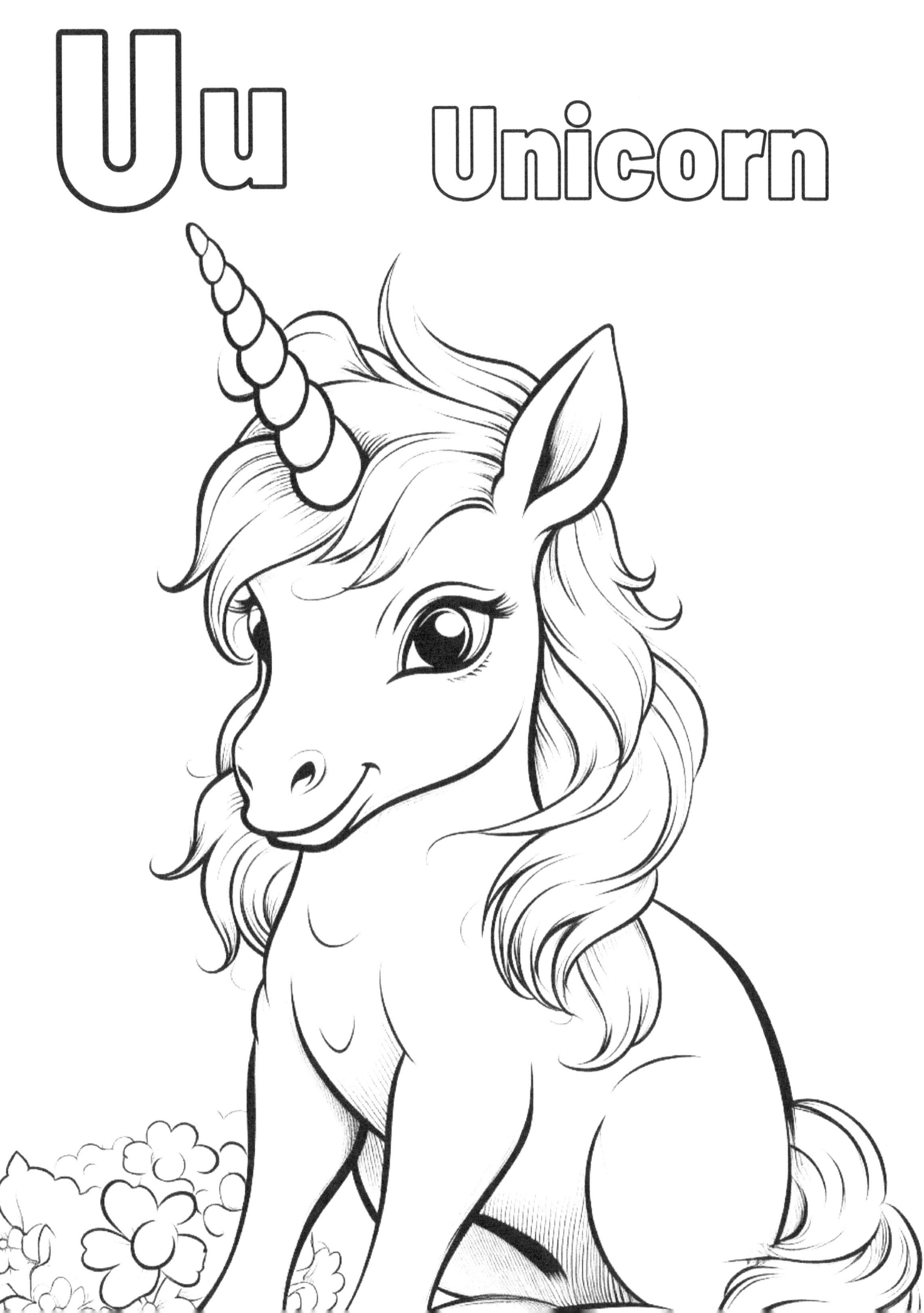

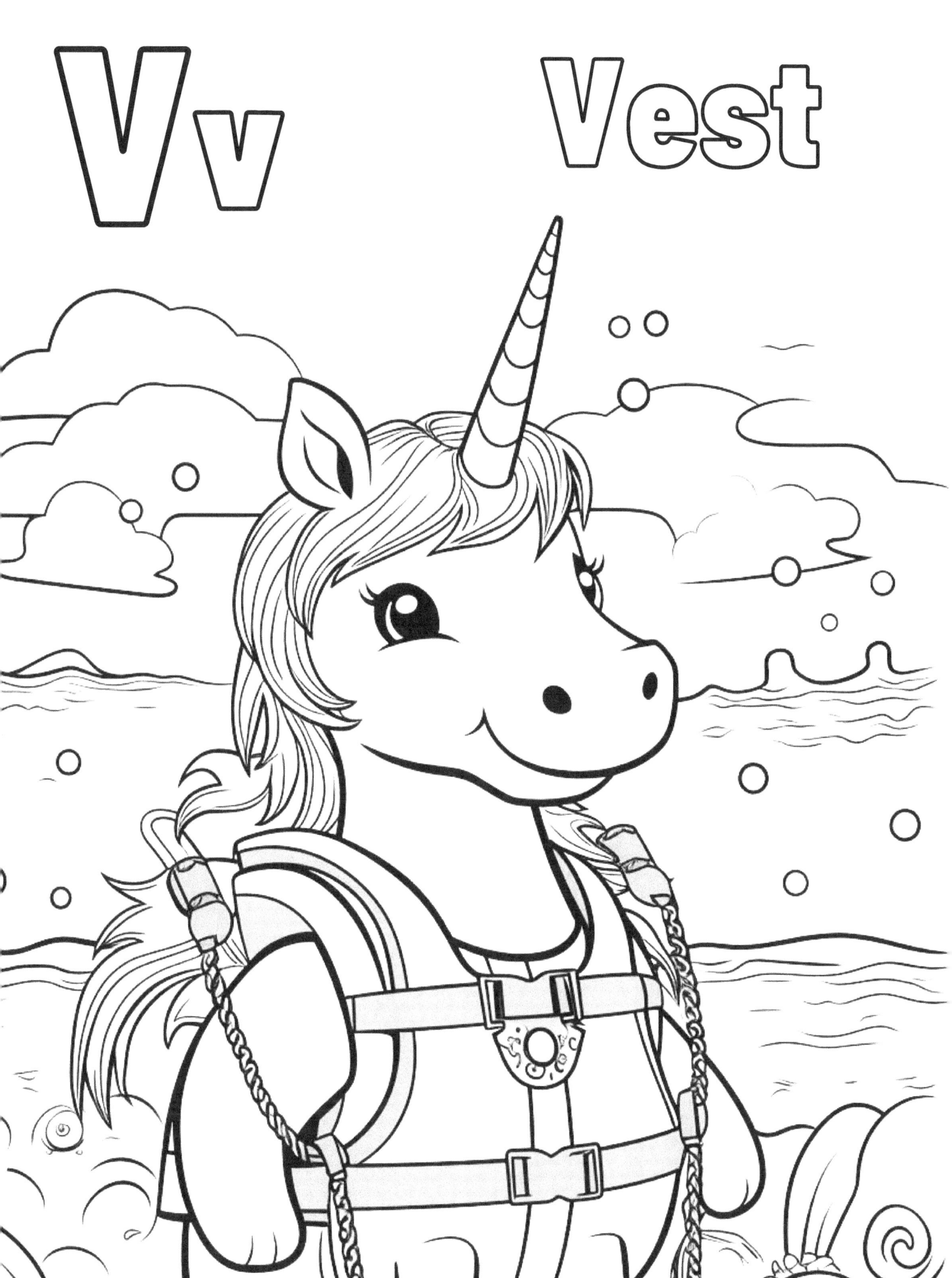

Ww Watch

X x   Xylophone

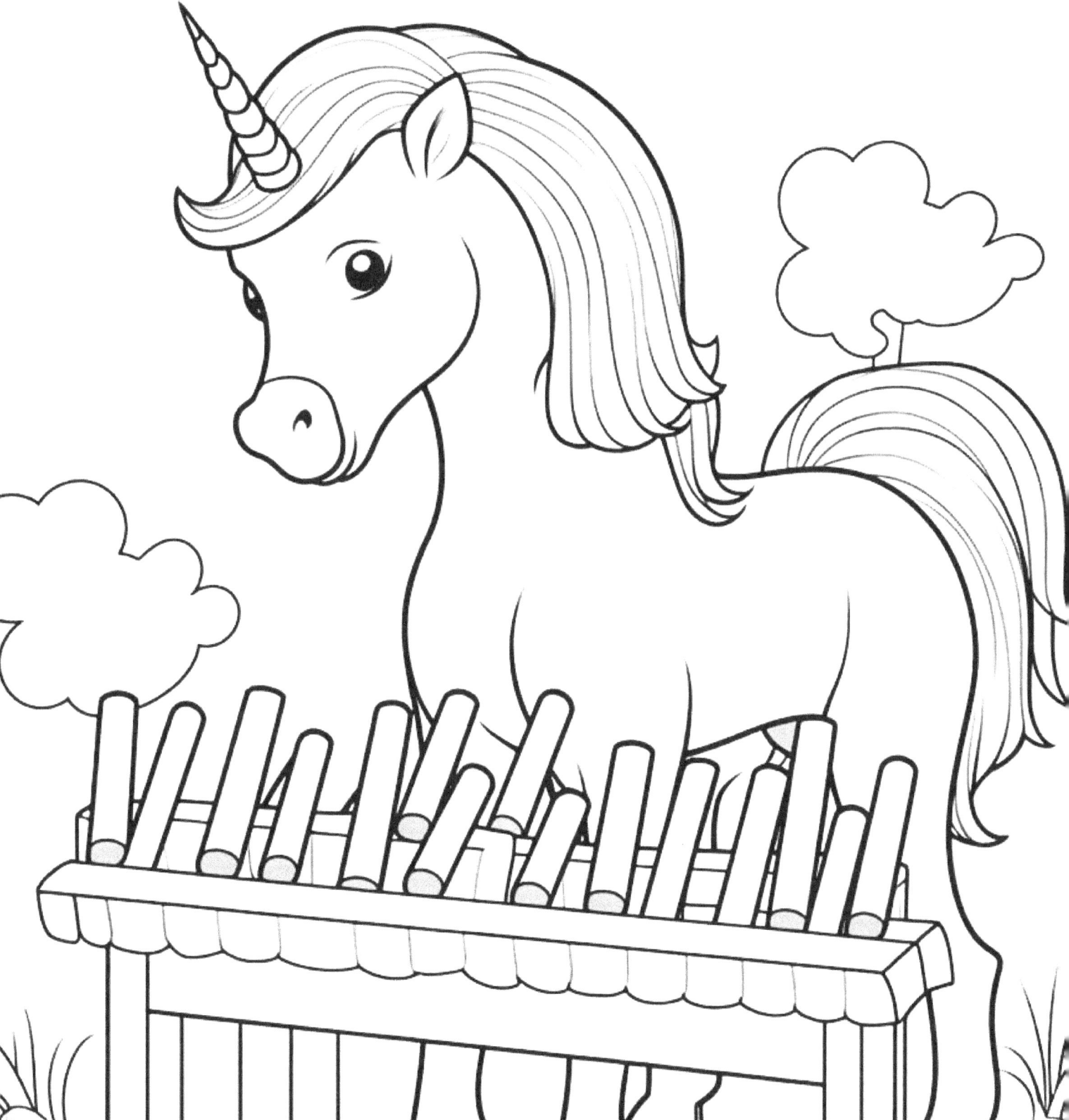

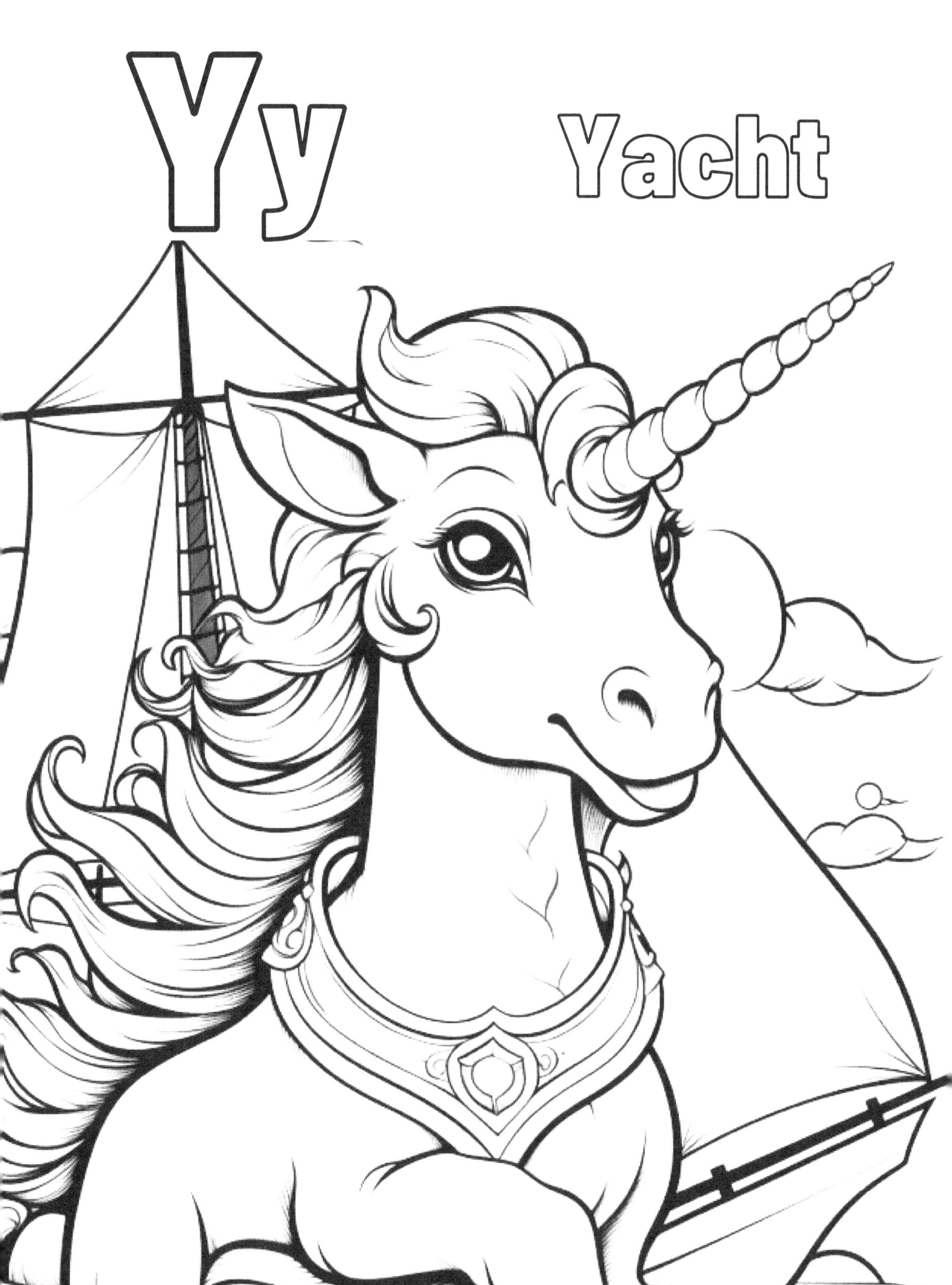

Zz   Zeppelin

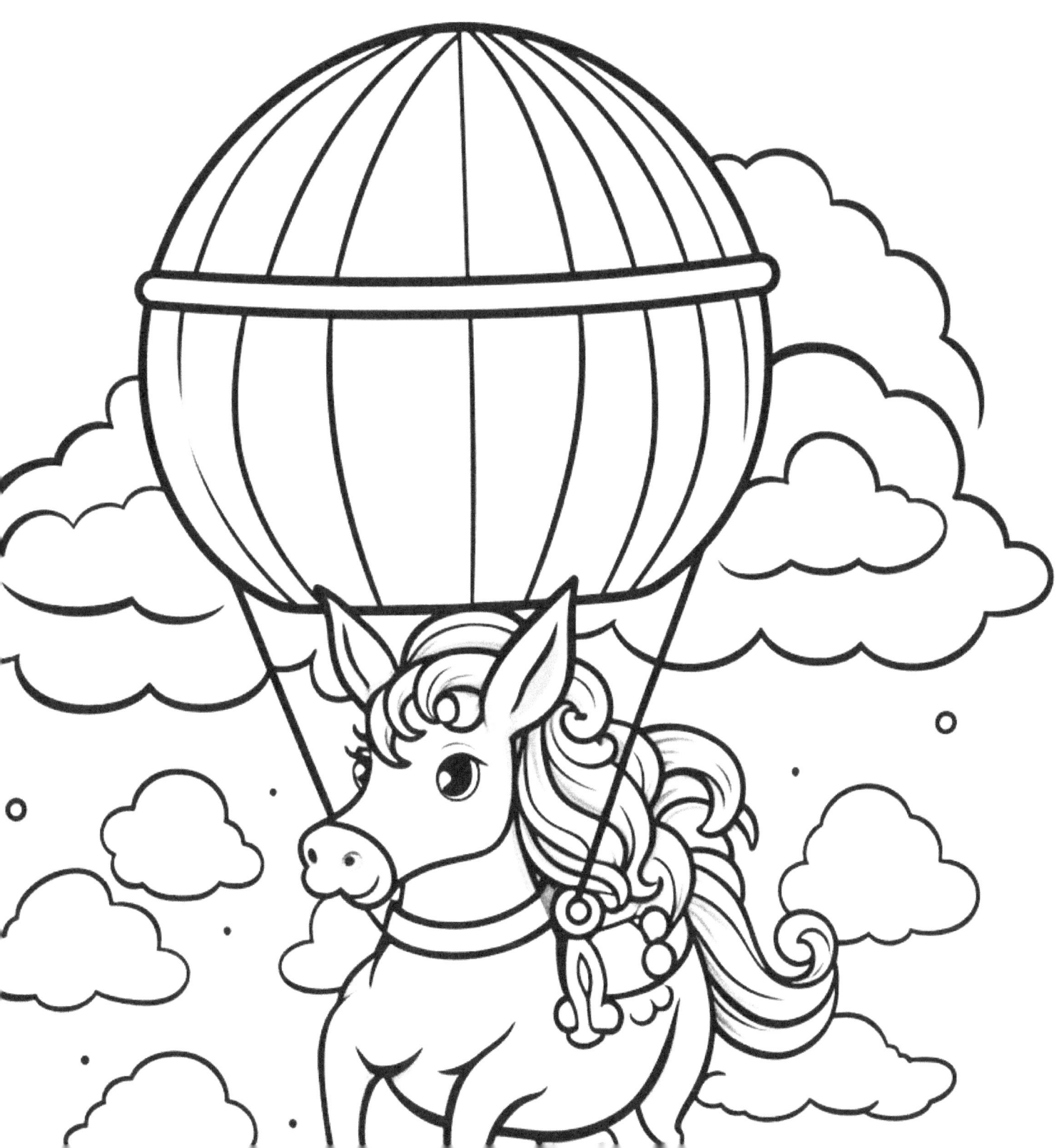

LET'S PRACTICE TOGETHER

A

LET'S PRACTICE TOGETHER

a

LET'S PRACTICE TOGETHER

B

LET'S PRACTICE TOGETHER

b

LET'S PRACTICE TOGETHER

C

LET'S PRACTICE TOGETHER

C

LET'S PRACTICE TOGETHER

D

LET'S PRACTICE TOGETHER

d

LET'S PRACTICE TOGETHER

E

LET'S PRACTICE TOGETHER

e

LET'S PRACTICE TOGETHER

F

LET'S PRACTICE TOGETHER

f

LET'S PRACTICE TOGETHER

G

LET'S PRACTICE TOGETHER

g

LET'S PRACTICE TOGETHER

H

LET'S PRACTICE TOGETHER

h

LET'S PRACTICE TOGETHER

LET'S PRACTICE TOGETHER

LET'S PRACTICE TOGETHER

J

LET'S PRACTICE TOGETHER

j

LET'S PRACTICE TOGETHER

K

LET'S PRACTICE TOGETHER

k

LET'S PRACTICE TOGETHER

L

LET'S PRACTICE TOGETHER

LET'S PRACTICE TOGETHER

M

LET'S PRACTICE TOGETHER

m

LET'S PRACTICE TOGETHER

N

LET'S PRACTICE TOGETHER

n

LET'S PRACTICE TOGETHER

0

LET'S PRACTICE TOGETHER

(0)

LET'S PRACTICE TOGETHER

P

LET'S PRACTICE TOGETHER

p

LET'S PRACTICE TOGETHER

Q

LET'S PRACTICE TOGETHER

q

LET'S PRACTICE TOGETHER

R

LET'S PRACTICE TOGETHER

r

LET'S PRACTICE TOGETHER

S

_____

_____

_____

_____

_____

_____

_____

_____

_____

_____

_____

_____

_____

LET'S PRACTICE TOGETHER

S

LET'S PRACTICE TOGETHER

T

LET'S PRACTICE TOGETHER

t

LET'S PRACTICE TOGETHER

U

LET'S PRACTICE TOGETHER

u

LET'S PRACTICE TOGETHER

V

LET'S PRACTICE TOGETHER

V

LET'S PRACTICE TOGETHER

W

LET'S PRACTICE TOGETHER

W

LET'S PRACTICE TOGETHER

X

_____

_____

_____

_____

_____

_____

_____

_____

_____

_____

_____

_____

_____

LET'S PRACTICE TOGETHER

X

LET'S PRACTICE TOGETHER

Y

_____

_____

_____

_____

_____

_____

_____

_____

_____

_____

_____

_____

_____

LET'S PRACTICE TOGETHER

y

LET'S PRACTICE TOGETHER

Z

LET'S PRACTICE TOGETHER

Z